contents

in association with:

Allan&Bath
Established 1898
www.allanandbath.co.uk

pictures: durdle door by kevin mitchell (front cover); dave taylor (top left); vicki mead (top right); rob rowe (bottom)

1

foreword

by dorset's nick dempsey, olympic sailing silver medallist

This has been, without a doubt, the best Olympic sailing event ever.

If you look back at the history of the Olympic Games, the other sailing events haven't even come close.

We knew Weymouth and Portland's sailing waters were good but this was the borough at its best and for that, we were lucky.

Not only did the sun shine for us but there were strong winds for racing and thousands of spectators turned out to create a unique stadium experience that none of us Olympic sailors have experienced before.

The Beijing Games was special and being able to celebrate that with everyone back home afterwards with an open-top bus parade through Weymouth and Portland was great.

But this time the whole county really got involved. It's been about more than just our achievement as sailors, it's really been about the whole area's achievement and, like the photography in this fantastic book, it's shown Weymouth, Portland and Dorset off at its best.

People will come back here not just because it's a nice place but because the people are nice and it's a friendly environment; that's what makes this whole thing so special.

It doesn't get any better than winning an Olympic medal in front of a home crowd.

We're lucky enough to train in Weymouth and Portland but to have been able to compete here at the Olympic Games is just unbelievable.

It was a once in a lifetime event, as was the open-top bus parade afterwards to show our thanks and appreciation for everyone's support.

These have been the real moments that we'll cherish forever and I'm delighted to be sharing that experience with you through the pages of this magnificent book.

nick dempsey rides the wind and waves to silver in the rs:x

west dorset

rolling hills and pasture, chocolate box villages and the birth of fossil hunting

The mighty Chesil Beach sweeps along west Dorset as the pride of the Jurassic Coast.

Pretty market towns and villages nestle on the beautiful countryside behind the shingle bank from West Bay to Portland.

The bustling market town of Bridport – dubbed 'Notting-Hill-on-Sea' – boasts a rich and colourful history on the meeting of the rivers Brit and Asker. Its citizens are rightly proud of its great rope and net making heritage; an industry which survives and prospers to this day.

Fishing boats bob in the harbour at West Bay, while beaches at Burton Bradstock and Eype are a short stroll away.

Visitors flock to the area for its fantastic walks and beaches as well as the rich cultural life and thriving arts and food scene.

The coast gives way to rolling countryside inland with 'chocolate box' villages, hamlets and small towns.

The pick include Powerstock, Netherbury and the undiscovered villages of the Marshwood Vale.

The Cobb is perhaps the best known landmark of the charming seaside resort of Lyme Regis on Dorset's border with Devon.

The imposing harbour wall has protected the town for centuries but also featured in writer John Fowles's classic novel The French Lieutenant's Woman – and the acclaimed film adaptation starring Meryl Streep.

But the Pearl of Dorset, as Lyme is known, is also famous for the fantastic fossils unearthed from its nearby cliffs with many breathtaking finds hanging in the Natural History Museum.

Pioneering fossil hunter Mary Anning's ghost still haunts the shoreline in the shape of the thousands of enthusiasts and amateur holiday makers who hope to strike a lucky find each year.

a mid-november sun sets beyond the harbour walls at lyme regis

picture: alan hill

■ west bay observation (left)
■ a stormy december shore at east cliff at west bay (below)

dawn shines over the mists around bridport and colmer's hill

picture: john nash (main); marie mears (top right)

february's evening sun lights lyme bay, seen from the fort on eggardon hill

picture: peter vincent

st catherine's chapel above abbotsbury, with the fleet and chesil beach beyond

the setting sun seen from the hilltop at st catherine's chapel

picture: kevin westmancott

ponies enjoy the warmth of the early morning november sun near colmer's hill

october sunshine at morecombelake, looking towards langdon hill

the old coastguard lookout near swyre, seen after sunset in january

■ looking down on the village of askerswell from the a35 between bridport and dorchester (below)

picture: terry dean (left); steve kemp (right)

the 'hidden lake' at little bredy

the cobb at lyme regis

picture: john fanning (left)

evening light warms the scene at charmouth beach, looking west towards lyme regis

fishing boats rest on the harbour bottom at low tide in lyme regis

a misty morning at bridport as the sun rises over chesil beach

portland

a rugged and time-ravaged island that became the centre of the sailing world

Travelling along the causeway to Portland gives you a chance to take a deep breath and fully switch off. 'The isle', as locals call it, has a unique sense of tranquillity that belies the busy community activity on Portland.

There are numerous social clubs, groups and clean-up days that show what a close-knit community the island is.

Popular with locals and more adventurous holidaymakers is Church Ope Cove on the east side of the island.

Leisurely minutes can turn into hours here, where brightly coloured beach huts characterise the perfectly formed cove of white pebbles.

The 12th century Rufus Castle and a pirates' graveyard provide plenty of distraction on the footpath down to Church Ope.

Portland Bill is probably the island's most famous landmark, along with nearby Pulpit Rock – an artificial stack of rocks left in the 1870s.

Also popular is the round-the-island coastal path, Tout Quarry sculpture park and Chesil Cove.

Development on the island has revamped Portland Harbour, creating a busy marina walkway and popular sitting out areas by the Boat That Rocked and at the Weymouth and Portland National Sailing Academy.

New homes have been built on Officers Field and a new academy for schoolchildren is being built at Southwell Business Park.

Whether it's the wild desolate winter beauty of Portland or its simple summer pleasures, the island has a bewitching effect on most people.

pulpit rock stands below a heavy sky as the sun goes down off portland

early-morning low tide at portland lighthouse

pictures: ian alcock (left); alan cox (right)

midnight in winter, the portland bill lighthouse stands on duty

a winter storm pounds the rocky coast of portland

a low winter sun lights the cloud and white horses as a storm blows through at portland bill

pulpit rock illuminated by the low evening sun

portland by night

fishing, family and fun on chesil beach

pictures: sue hogben (left); garry wells (right)

looking down from high on portland, over fortuneswell, along the curve of chesil beach and across the harbour to weymouth and beyond

weymouth

characterful resort with elegant georgian terraces and swathes of stunning sands

Weymouth is a lively town that doesn't just fall back on its natural beauty and rich history to charm people.
It is a sociable place where the continental way of life is easy to lead, with an abundance of sitting out areas by the harbour and the seafront.

Residents and tourists alike are never far away from a water view, be it Weymouth harbour, the seafront or the jaw-dropping sweep of pebbles that make up Chesil Beach.

A major road improvement scheme and a new £3.5million viewing tower mean that the face of the town is changing rapidly.

The relief road has shaved minutes off journey times into town, making Weymouth more accessible.
The town is thought to be the first port at which the Black Death came to England and counts Sir Christopher Wren as its most famous MP.
The legacy of King George III is visible all over Weymouth.

The discerning royal holidayed in Weymouth on 14 occasions between 1789 and 1805, making the town one of the first modern tourist destinations.
While Weymouth has many coastal charms, its countryside is equally alluring.

Abbotsbury is a chocolate-box village full of honey-coloured cottages, while nearby Hardy's Monument is perfect for admiring the rural beauty of Dorset from 72ft.

The green spaces of Radipole Nature Reserve and Lodmoor Country Park and Nature Reserve are perfect for twitching or for some quiet contemplation.
Wonderful Weymouth has many dimensions.

weymouth's sweeping seafront esplanade reflected at low tide

heading between the masts with the rods at sunrise

moonlight reflected in weymouth quay as the lifeboat floats on its mooring

one of the beach donkeys, a little shy about his awards...

picture: stuart robinson

reflections in the early hours of an april morning near weymouth town bridge

picture: andy harris

the secret lagoon, near chesil beach

sea mist closes in on portland harbour, as seen from old castle road

sunrise at osmington mills

pictures: ian alcock (left), kathryn glynn (right)

sunset at osmington mills

an idyllic summer scene looking across weymouth bay, paragliders over the white horse, yachts leisurely motoring by

pictures: andy harris (main), karl watson (top)

a woolly-hilled 'sheepscape' above ringstead bay looking towards portland

■ even in october sunshine can bring out the swimmers and the sun bathers (left)

■ bonfire night fireworks over the pavilion and the condor ferry (right)

weymouth's bustling harbour

picture: paul waddilove (bottom); kevin westmancott (top right)

full throttle in weymouth's beach motocross

inspired by monet... bridge and lilies at bennetts' water garden, weymouth

a winter sunset seen from osmington mills

dorchester

dorset's county town with a history dating back thousands of years

As befits the county town, Dorchester is a place steeped in history.

From its entrenched association with Thomas Hardy to the Roman history scattered about the town, you are never far away from reminders of Dorchester's heritage.

It was known as Durnovaria by Romans, who settled in the area already featuring the prominent Iron Age landmarks of Maumbury Rings and Maiden Castle.

But for many the town will always be 'Casterbridge', the fictional town based on Dorchester created by Hardy – who was born at nearby Higher Bockhampton and lived in the town at Max Gate.

As well as a literary heritage that also celebrates the poet William Barnes, there is a notable legal history that is still there for all to see at the Old Crown Court and Cells.

The court was the setting for the 1834 trial of the Tolpuddle Martyrs – farm labourers who had sown the seed, in Dorset, for the origins of the trades union movement.

With Prince Charles' model development at Poundbury stretching away to the west of the town, Dorchester also serves as a hub for surrounding communities such as Charminster, Charlton Down, Puddletown, Broadmayne and Crossways.

As the ongoing construction work at Poundbury expands the town's reach, the centre of Dorchester is also the focus of two major redevelopment projects.

Work is well underway in a bid to transform the former Eldridge Pope Brewery site into a modern development featuring cafes, restaurants, shops, hotels and flats, while there are also plans for a major retail project on the site of the Charles Street car parks in the town centre.

maiden castle, south west of dorchester

swans, and family, on the river frome

picture: simon porter

the giant's view of cerne abbas

staying the course at milborne st andrew

late summer sunrise, seen from greys bridge over the frome at dorchester

a snow-covered seven acre coppice near portesham

picture: brian crump

all is quiet at dorchester's roman town house in a fresh fall of december snow

picture: kevin westmancott

the creator of casterbridge, thomas hardy

the tolpuddle martyrs discuss the beginnings of the trades union movement, in south walks, dorchester

purbeck

gateway to the jurassic coast, saturated with human and geological history

The Isle of Purbeck has long been a jewel in Dorset's glittering crown. Its 60 square miles hold countless clues to our island's cultural heritage, while its stunning cliffs stand as testament to millions of years of the evolution of life on earth.

These towering cliffs, rising in the east and marking the start of the spectacular Jurassic coast walk, are packed with fossil forests, providing a snapshot into prehistoric life.

The coast also boasts world-renowned landmarks such as Durdle Door and still-quarried beds of Portland and Purbeck limestone, which still play a vital role in the area's economic history.

The beautiful Victorian resort town of Swanage and Wareham's historic quayside and bustling market provide the region's commercial centres.

Where once the Purbeck economy depended largely on agriculture and maritime pursuits, today the focus has shifted to tourism.

A number of stunning attractions are based in the area, although none as great as Purbeck itself.

Much of it is designated an Area of Outstanding Natural Beauty.

The scenery has long captivated Purbeck visitors, who have eagerly explored its country lanes and hilltop pathways.

A popular way to take in the sights is from one of the carriages of the hugely evocative steam trains of the volunteer Swanage Railway.

And the gateway to Purbeck? Without doubt the ruins of historic Corfe Castle.

Fortified since before the Norman invasion, the oldest parts date from the 11th century and it served as a royal treasure storehouse and even a prison before becoming a casualty of the Civil War in 1646 as it fell from Royalist hands.

Even the most leisurely visit into the Isle of Purbeck reveals a natural treasure beyond compare.

blue skies and flat sea, an idyllic september scene in worbarrow bay

the sun rises to start burning off the mist on the river frome at wareham

swanage old pier

picture: marc paull

a high viewpoint on bats head, seen from the south west coast path along the jurassic coast

58

■ a 'flying' fishing boat sails past old harry rocks (below)

pictures: billy connolly (left); kevin mitchell (right)

the globe at swanage colourfully lit as the sun sets beyond

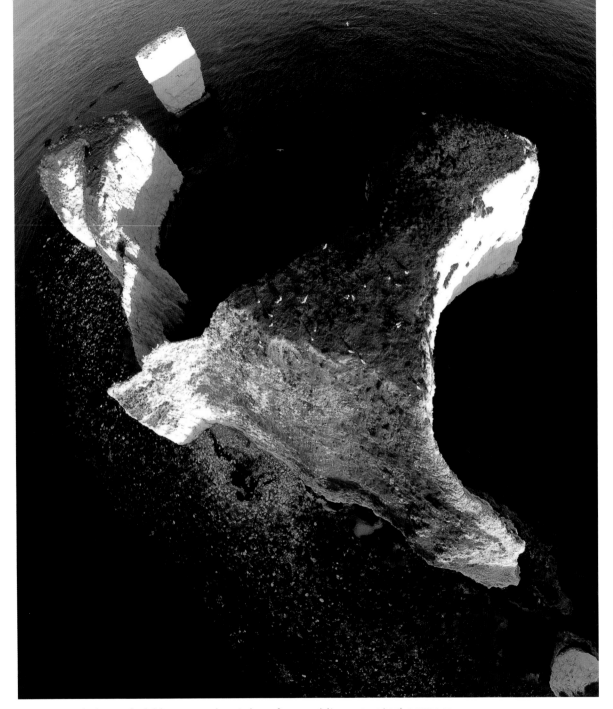

an unusual view of old harry rocks, taken from a kite-mounted camera

■ star trails above grange arch at creech (below)

pictures: andrew holder (left); graham fry (right)

winter sunrise at corfe castle

peacefully grazing sheep belie the historic turmoil of the corfe castle ruins beyond

picture: garry wells

corfe castle eerily emerges from the morning mists

a clearly exposed ammonite at kimmeridge (left)

the anvil point lighthouse at durlston (below)

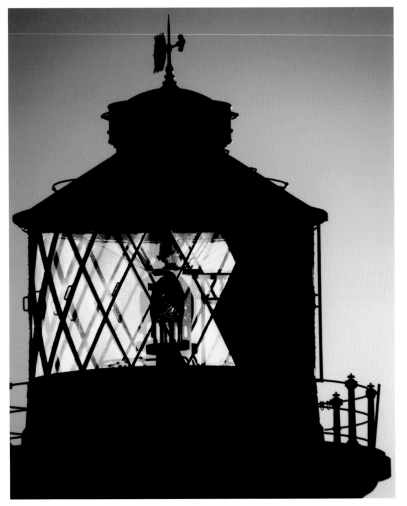

the tide has turned at kimmeridge, below clavell tower

pictures: marc paull (left); anne elford (top right); milly haines (bottom right)

looking down the steps to durdle door with portland on the horizon

■ new year's day dawns at bats
head (below)

a boat is well anchored at chapmans pool

pictures: mike sutton (left); andy smith (right)

waves splash up onto dancing ledge

taking in the view at white nothe, looking east towards durdle door and lulworth

pictures: heather snow (left); andy legg (right)

an unusual view, from dungy head, looking west over st oswald's bay to the back of durdle door and bats head

an adonis blue butterfly enjoys the flora above durdle door

picture: mary dorey (left)

light shines through durdle door

dorset's olympics and paralympics

when a sailing fleet brought the world to weymouth and portland

The sun shone, the wind blew and thousands of cheering spectators flocked to watch fiercely competitive racing on Dorset's Olympic and Paralympic waters.

When the eyes of the world turned to Weymouth and Portland, the host venue for the sailing competitions for the London 2012 Games did not disappoint. Turquoise waters glistened as the world's best sailors raced to overcome the elements, and each other, to turn years of work into Olympic and Paralympic glory. The Jurassic coastline provided a natural amphitheatre for the first-ever ticketed spectator site in Olympic sailing history.

Thunderous cheers from the crowds at Nothe Gardens, and along the coast, spurred on Star sailors Iain Percy and Andrew Simpson as they claimed silver and began Team GB's five-strong medal haul. Rule Britannia rang out loud as Ben Ainslie won his historic fourth gold medal and became the most

successful Olympic sailor in The Games' history. Weymouth's windsurfer Nick Dempsey won silver and the hearts of the crowd when he swam ashore after his medal race to hug his three-year-old son Thomas. Silver for both Britain's 470 dinghy teams - Hannah Mills and Saskia Clark, and Luke Patience and Stuart Bithell - ended the Olympic sailing regatta on a high. Weymouth Carnival Day celebrated their achievements when they starred in an open-top bus parade. World-class racing returned to Portland Harbour for the Paralympic sailing regatta and Britain won its first ever medals in the sport when 2.4mR sailor Helena Lucas won gold and Alex Rickham and Niki Birrell achieved Skud-18 bronze.

The Sonar team narrowly missed out on another bronze due to a controversial penalty.

Like their Olympic counterparts, the ParalympicsGB sailing athletes proudly rose to the occasion of the home Games and made history on Dorset waters.

paul goodison competing in the men's laser fleet

'they've made me angry and you don't want to make me angry'... ben ainslie celebrates gold

ben ainslie watched by thousands

saskia clark and hannah mills celebrate after winning silver in the women's 470

■ saskia clark and hannah mills fly the flag (right)

■ hannah mills and saskia clark with their treasure (below)

saskia clark and hannah mills power ahead of china and australia in the women's 470

PATIENCE
BITHELL

jubilant luke patience and stuart bithell celebrate after winning silver in the men's 470

luke patience and stuart bithell manoeuvre at the start of the men's 470

■ iain percy and andrew simpson powering through in the star fleet (right)

■ team gb match race girls: poole's own lucy macgregor, annie lush and kate macgregor (below)

paul goodison before coming in second in his last race of the day

iain percy and andrew simpson battle their way out of the pack at the start of a star class race

■ nick dempsey is interviewed
after winning his silver medal (below)

nick dempsey on top of the world after taking rs:x men's silver

nick dempsey works the wind ahead of the pack in the rs:x men's class

bryony shaw in the women's rs:x

ali young pushes her laser radial to the limit

laser radial race

britain's 49er sailors ben rhodes and stevie morrison

finn racing with hms bulwark as the backdrop; security was reassuringly substantial

the men's 470s round the mark

the duchess of cambridge, kate middleton, enjoys a joke with members of team gb

prime minister david cameron with ben ainslie, team gb sailing manager stephen park and andrew simpson

■ crowds show their appreciation for the weymouth and portland spectator ambassadors as they parade along the esplanade (left)

■ the olympics brought the 'brit' out in all of us (right)

as excitement grew all vantage points were filled, including on the rocks below nothe fort... at low tide

the nothe viewing area attracted thousands of ticketed spectators

spectators enjoyed many vantage points, here the nothe and the sea life tower

weymouth carnival - team gb sailors parade along weymouth seafront in an open top bus

■ the sonar class fleet (left)

alexandra rickham and niki birrell pass the fort on portland harbour breakwater

helena lucas celebrates winning britain's first ever paralympic sailing gold medal

■ helena lucas catches up on her gold medal news (right) and with her precious metal (below right)

helena lucas racing to an historic triumph in the 2.4mr class

helena lucas rounds the mark in the hunt for a first-ever gb paralympic sailing gold medal

■ alexandra rickham and niki birrell show off their treasure

alexandra rickham and niki birrell work their boat on their way to third in the skud-18 class

alexandra rickham and niki birrell fly the flag as they power their way to bronze in the skud-18 class

john robertson, hannah stodel and stephen thomas fight for the lead in the sonar class

john robertson, hannah stodel and stephen thomas powering downwind in the sonar class

north dorset

ancient earthworks, historic market towns and countless festivals and fairs

To visit North Dorset is to visit an ancient and beautiful land of picturesque villages with thatched cottages and quaint pubs.

The area's heritage ranges from the mysterious pagan rings of Knowlton to the Christian ruins of Shaftesbury Abbey.

Historic market towns are set around the sweeping chalk downland of Cranborne Chase and the fertile basin of the Blackmore Vale.

The northernmost town is Gillingham, home to a Stone Age barrow, and a Saxon cross shaft dating from the ninth century.

Blandford, rebuilt in the Georgian style by the Bastard Brothers after the devastating fire of 1731, is today also home to the Royal School of Signals.

Visitors to Shaftesbury can take in Gold Hill, a famously steep and cobbled street, and a history that includes the death of King Canute.

The lively market town Sturminster Newton sits in the middle of historic dairy farming country, and has a working mill and an annual cheese festival.

The numerous attractive villages include Okeford Fitzpaine, home to many timber-framed cottages, and Stalbridge, which has a medieval 30ft high market cross.

Walkers and cyclists can enjoy the seven-mile long North Dorset Trailway, with spectacular views of Hambledon Hill, home to a prehistoric hill fort.

North Dorset is home to countless festivals from the Filly Loo, an ancient dance beside Ashmore Pond to mark the Summer Solstice, to the Great Dorset Steam Fair.

summer's evening light glows through the arches of a bridge at blandford forum

perfect reflections in the mill pond at sturminster newton

flying high over shaftesbury, one of britain's highest towns

on the move at the great dorset steam fair

smoking silhouettes of steam engines at the steam fair

dawn illuminates the early morning mists at tarrant keyneston (below)

a frosty sunrise on the stour looking towards langton long

picture: rob cullum (left); jason pizzey (right)

a winter scene surrounds the mill at sturminster newton

a field of pink poppies near blandford

pictures: margaret hamilton (left); michelle prince (right)

a clear bright winter's day on hambledon hill

first light bathes a scene of freshly fallen snow, looking towards bulbarrow hill from woolland

st peter's church in pimperne wears a winter coat

east dorset

lush river valleys and rolling landscape mix with a rich historical background

East Dorset's towns, villages and beautiful country surrounds combine to make it a hit with visitors and residents alike.

Wimborne Minster, a market town caught between the rivers Allen and Stour, is a particular favourite with a rich history dating back to Saxon times.

The 11th century Minster, with its famed Chained Library, draws in tourists, who find themselves enchanted by the independent shops and wide choice of cafes, restaurants and pubs.

Children are easily entertained thanks to the Priest's House Museum and the model town. Just a short drive away lies Kingston Lacy, a 17th century house now owned by the National Trust, and Badbury Rings, a spectacular Iron Age hill fort.

Each October there is also Wimborne Food Festival to showcase local produce and whet appetites.

Nearby Ferndown hosts an annual carnival, entertainment at the Barrington Centre all year round and a selection of shops.

A short way up the A31 is Verwood, a town which has grown up remarkably over the last 20 years.

It now has its own community centre, cafe and meeting place in The Hub, a small group of shops and facilities and a number of first and middle schools.

Popular days out include Moors Valley Country Park, Avon Heath Country Park and Honeybrook Farm, which showcase the area's natural environment and farming background.

poppies in bloom at cranborne

iconic east dorset view, badbury rings

pictures: david rogers (left); paul mckay (right)

directions by cottages at witchampton

119

a sunny morning bursts through the conifers at colehill plantation

autumn arrives at the beech avenue near kingston lacy outside wimborne

winter mists on the stour,
near the bridge house at longham
(left)

horses graze in the early morning mist at the river stour

picture: karyn cuglietta (main), robert burton (top)

beyond wimborne minster the coming sunrise prepares to burn back the winter mist at eye bridge, on the stour

picture: andrew bannister

a sharp morning at badbury rings

picture: karen arnold

dawn arrives at knowlton church

spring lambs at merley hall farm, the towers of wimborne minster beyond

■ late afternoon during harvest time on north farm, horton (left)

■ aerial view of kingston lacy house (below, thanks to gary ellson of bournemouth helicopters)

picture: bob thomas (top right)

horton folly lit by a january sunset

poole

from tribal beginnings to a thriving natural harbour and commercial port

Ancient Poole has a brand new attraction, the world-class Twin Sails Bridge.

The town's second harbour crossing is the culmination of decades of desire and its opening was marked with considerable pride, special events and a visit by the Princess Royal.

Spanning the Back Water Channel between the town and Hamworthy, when the lit triangular sails lift at night the spectacular sight is a tourist attraction in its own right.

It kick-starts the regeneration of the old town and lower Hamworthy, however as new developments spring up, there is still plenty of old Poole to explore. The ever popular quayside fronts one of the world's largest natural harbours with a total coastline of 100km, heaven for yachtsmen and wildlife lovers with the National Trust's jewel of Brownsea Island to visit. Reaching back into the town are smugglers' alleys and a network of lanes to walk with historic buildings ranging from Georgian charm to old pubs covered in local Carter's tiles, forerunner of world famous Poole Pottery.

At the entrance to the harbour lies one of the most expensive spits of sand in the world at Sandbanks, whose Millionaires' Row seafront homes are a celebrity magnet.

A whole programme of special events takes place each year from the British Beach Polo Championships to cars, motorbikes and family fun on the beach and the quay.

And after all the excitement there are plenty of places to relax and enjoy the sunshine, including family-friendly Poole Park and Canford Cliff's glorious Compton Acres gardens.

poole's gleaming new twin sails bridge opened to the public in april 2012

a runner passes the crowds exploring the twin sails bridge on its public opening day

poole lifting bridge has served the town well for over 80 years

sunset at low tide in poole harbour

pictures: david money (main) and andrew thomas (right)

an impressive view over poole harbour from a transatlantic airline: studland left of the entrance, poole to the right, sandbanks ferry halfway between

echoes of a bygone era as a tall ship towers over poole quay

picture: sue white

reflections as christmas arrives at poole quay

one of brownsea island's red squirrels

late summer sun sets across poole harbour

speeding by hamworthy park in february morning light

pictures: phil jackson

an early summer's morning at branksome beach, looking towards old harry and the purbecks

poole harbour shore, frozen during february 2012; hints of warmer days to come – snowdrops in poole park

fresh december snow at upton house

jet ski coming in to land at poole

picture: michelle luther (left); jenna giles-bodilly (right)

wet sand and puddles, splashing time at low tide

silhouettes from evening hill, looking across sandbanks to old harry (top left)

low sun, low tide (bottom left)

the former cube gallery at bournemouth & poole college (right)

picture: andrew ward (bottom left)

autumn in upton country park

bournemouth

miles of soft golden sands on the edge of a beautiful south-facing bay

Bournemouth is best known for its seven miles of curving golden sands but there is so much more to the resort than its award-winning beaches.

The borough boasts 21 conservation areas and 842 hectares (2,080 acres) of manicured parks and gardens.

With excellent transport links to major cities, Bournemouth is within easy reach of the New Forest National Park, the Isle of Wight and stunning Purbeck. In recent years the town has swapped its blue rinse image to arguably become the clubbing capital of the South.

Renowned for many attractions, including its seafront Oceanarium and cliff-top Russell-Cotes art gallery and museum, Bournemouth is one of the UK's top holiday destinations with an average of 7.7 hours of sunshine on summer days.

Since the Bournemouth International Centre opened, the town has become a popular conference and live entertainment venue.

With its own university and airport, the tourism industry continues to be a major source of employment.

But the town also relies heavily on income generated from the thousands of foreign students who set up temporary home in the town every year.

Insurance companies have also given the town their stamp of approval.

Bournemouth's population is expected to swell to almost 180,000 by 2033 as more families move to the coast and opt for the undeniable charms of a life by the seaside.

a spectacular christmas eve sunrise at bournemouth pier

surf, spray and silhouette along the seafront

pictures: ricky bedding (top & bottom left), steve tydeman (right)

a lone boarder paddles by boscombe beach

thousands flock to the beaches when the temperatures rise

a sandcastle is left to defend bournemouth beach after the crowds have gone

wind and weather blow over southbourne beach and hengistbury head

a beautiful sunrise over mudeford, christchurch harbour and the heather on hengistbury head

first light on the groyne at hengistbury head

picture: roger burton

evening sees a lone fisherman at hengistbury head, as dramatic clouds gather to the east

friday family fiesta with the fireworks at bournemouth pier

pictures: sam warsiewicz (left); steve wisdom (right)

'living sculpture' silhouetted on bournemouth beach

an early november morning, the promenade lights sparkle as the dawn glow emerges in the east

picture: marcia robberts

the tide rolls in below bournemouth pier on a winter's night

■ first lights at boscombe's award winning pier (below)

■ a dark and windy day near bournemouth pier (bottom)

sun, sea and sand sparkle as a new day begins at bournemouth pier

pictures: kasia novak (left); luke bayliss (top right); sedat ozkanca (bottom right)

monochrome morning at boscombe pier

reflections on a sunny walk along the river stour in throop

winter colours on bournemouth seafront

christchurch

an ancient saxon settlement
where two rivers meet

The Saxon borough of Christchurch boasts a rich history that has kept visitors returning for hundreds of years.

Sandwiched between two rivers, Christchurch was formerly known as Twynham – a fort built on the orders of Alfred the Great against the Vikings.

The 11th century Priory Church stands majestically in the middle of the town, with rumours and stories from its long history still circulating among residents.

At the end of the 13th century, the priory was sold to King Edward I, making Christchurch a royal manor. It was stripped of its assets by Henry VIII in the Dissolution, but following a plea from local people led by John Draper, the last Prior of Christchurch, the building was spared, making it the longest parish church in the country, larger than some cathedrals.

Christchurch harbour, into which both the Rivers Avon and Stour flow, was once the scene of a thriving fishing industry before its importance declined as it became inaccessible to vessels of a large draught. And for many generations, the main industry in Christchurch was smuggling, a practice which in 1784 led to the locally famed Battle of Mudeford.

Today, many historical landmarks, including Place Mill near the bandstand on Christchurch Quay and Christchurch Castle in the town centre, have been preserved as part of the borough's rich heritage.

swans approach hopeful of food in freezing february temperatures on the river stour

an aerial 'flotilla' escorts a racing boat back to harbour at the end of the day

pictures: andy beeson (left); ken ames (right)

tranquillity at mudeford, as storm clouds build out at sea

a heron glides over christchurch harbour, a haven for wildlife

picture: roger burton

the sun rises behind grasses overlooking christchurch harbour

frozen light and lines at mudeford

picture: rachel mccormick

a frozen pool captures the warm colours of a winter sunset at wick village

picture: rob cherry

■ lobster pots at sunset on mudeford quay (left)

■ the day's swansong glows across christchurch harbour at mudeford (right)

people stroll along the river bank as the bandstand sits, hushed, at the end of the day

pictures: rita simmonds (left); sophie rolt (top left); richard swainson (right)

a fishing boat heads out past mudeford quay on a dawn low tide

september's sunrise glows over mudeford beach huts